TO
YELLOWSTONE
PARK
AND
BACK

BY
IRENE ANGUS

Edited by
Dora Lou Southern

Acknowledgements

In putting a book together,
as in life,
we are always assisted by caring people.
I have been greatly assisted
by my husband Don,
for his loving support
and my family
Steve and Renee, for all their encouragement
and our son Dwight,
whose patience and computer skills
made the recreation
of this journal possible.
Also many thanks to Ann Brinn Ward
and Dick Peterson for their advice
and
their generous help with editing.

I thank you all.

Introduction

❦

Dear Reader,

This is a personal journal and was not written with distribution in mind. However, it is too interesting not to be shared. It is an adventure as seen through Miss Irene Angus' eyes. It was written by my mother's cousin and came to me through my sister who cared for Irene in her retired years. In attempting to reconstruct her original book, I have taken liberties with the font, numbered the pages, and made some minor changes; but, all in all, the pages are laid out and reproduced as they appear in her journal. She used a typewriter of the day to type her pages, and I think she would have liked having a font choice. Of course photos were taken with whatever lighting was available, and post cards and pictures scanned with varying success.

There are two notes of historical interest. First, in 1903, a mere 26 years before Irene's trip, Horatio Nelson Jackson, the subject of Ken Burns' documentary entitled "Horatio's Drive" (aired on PBS in 2005), tells of an arduous "race" to be the first to drive a car from California to New York. Much of the journey was over really non-existing roads, and it adds a dimension to the kind of roads these ladies must have traveled. Second, the trip by Irene, Mickey, and Lucy took place the summer before the stock market crash in the fall of 1929. Had it been planned for only a short time later, it would never have taken place. Of course Irene and Lucy, being teachers, had planned to be back in time for the school year to begin.

It has been my great pleasure to work on this project. I hope Irene would approve of the effort and the results. She obviously enjoyed her trip as evidenced by her written account. You can almost hear the excitement in her voice as you read her journal. In the book Irene often says, "I wonder why". That was part of her nature; and once she found out "why", she was so pleased to use and to share her knowledge.

With sharing in mind,
Dora Lou Southern
(second cousin to the author)

June 2006

From the Travel Journal
of Irene Angus

Irene Angus
1900 – 1974
Teacher

To Yellowstone Park And Back

A Journal
July 20th — August 12th
1929

Irene Angus
Lucy Amborski
Michaelyn Amborski

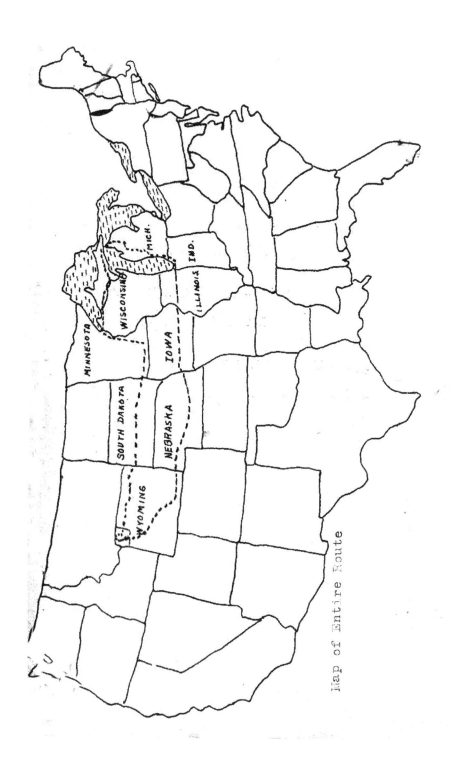

Map of Entire Route

SATURDAY — JULY 20th

We left home [Gaylord, MI] at 10:30. The speedometer stood at 18260. We started north on We had a detour around Wolverine that was rather rough and sandy.

The weather was great, bright, sunny and cool.

Gypsy Weather

When there's a yellow sun on the hill
And a wind as light as a feather
And the clouds frisk gaily, as young clouds will,
Oh, then it is gypsy weather.
That's the weather to travel in,
With the sun and the wind against the skin,
No matter how glad to rest you've been
You must go when it's gypsy weather.

- Mary Caroline Davies

This is the map of our routes through Michigan. The arrows indicate the direction we were going and x's indicate the places in which we stayed all night.

We ate our lunch in the State Park at Cheboygan. Mrs. Amborski had sent some chicken and mother an apple pie.

We missed the 2:00 ferry by a very narrow margin so had to wait for the one at 3:00. We drove out to the park and waited a while and then went back down town and bought some things for supper.

We crossed on the ferry "Straits of Mackinaw". It was rough — the deck came up and hit the bottom of your feet when you walked. It was fun to stand in the prow of the boat.

There were several grain boats like this going from Lake Michigan to Lake Huron.

There are many seagulls on the Straits. Some follow the ferries across. These were just over the side of the boat at St.Ignace.

We took US 31 north out of St.Ignace. Castle Rock is a short distance out on this road.

We soon came to which was to be our route for many miles.

We stopped and cooked and ate supper at about 5:30 at a place called Millers Lodge. We had hot boiled potatoes and lettuce salad, with bananas for dessert.

I think that Millers Lodge started out in life as a lumber camp, but there was a filling station there and sort of a hunting lodge. They had several owls, also wolves, foxes, and a raccoon, in rough cages.

Owls are baleful looking creatures. They have queer eye-lids.

We drove on after supper. We saw a heron beside the road in a swampy place.

We also saw a large hawk in a tree.

We stayed all night at Blaney. We had a fire in the wood stove. It felt good. We had good beds and a fine night's sleep. We were 156 miles from home.

SUNDAY - JULY 21st

We got up at 6:00 and got breakfast on the wood stove. Then we drove on to Manistique where the girls went to church, and I went to a garage where I had the rod that goes between the lights wired together and a new valve put in a tire.

We saw this bear on the way to Manistique. He was at a corner filling station. He walked and walked the pole and always stepped over the chain the same way.

A little way out of Manistique, we turned off the road and drove five miles over very rough road to see a big spring called Kitch-Iti-Kip-Pi. It is some three hundred feet in diameter and completely surrounded by swamp timber except for the outlet which winds away among these trees. The water from a distance is a peculiar green. The boy took us out on the raft. There are holes in the raft through which one can look through into the water. The water is so clear that one can see a coin on bottom forty feet below. The water boils up from the bottom all the time making queer pictures with the sand.

At the raft landing

Looking across and to the right from landing

The raft on the spring

*In the water on the side of the spring oppo-
site the landing*

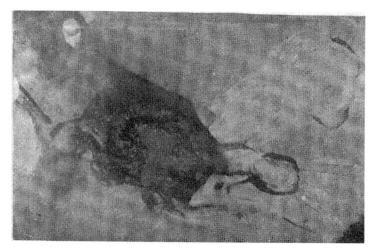

Sand seething up on the bottom of the spring

We ate our dinner at the Delta County Park on the Fishdam River. We got into the iron country in the afternoon. We drove for about twenty miles in Wisconsin then back again into Michigan.

Lucy treated us to a good dinner at a restaurant in Iron River. Then we turned our watches back an hour and drove on.

As the sun was setting we drove into Iron County Park on Golden Lake. Virgin hardwood and hemlock, beautiful lake. We stayed but a few minutes and then went on. I liked it there.

It grew very dark and we drove on and on through the woods. There were no settlements and it seemed a long time before we reached the next town which was Watersmeet.

We inquired for the best place for us to stay and were directed to the hotel. As we drove up and parked in front of the building the proprietress was just ejecting an intoxicated man. When she had finished, Lucy went in and asked if we could stay there. We could.

We carried our bags upstairs and she took us to a room; but there was already a man in it. So she parked us on a davenport in the hall while she ejected him. While waiting for him to move she helped another man to find his room as he was far too bewildered to find it alone. She also informed an inquirer that so-and-so was no longer there as he was in jail.

Soon our room was ready. We washed, locked our door, and slept the sleep of the Just or some similar sleep until morning. We had traveled 243 miles.

The Kelly Hotel

The account above does not sound as though it was a good place to stay — but it was. It was clean, the service was efficient, and the proprietress (who was certainly never born a Kelly, but probably came of a long line of inn-keeping Germans) was so very calm and capable that even under those circumstances one was quite certain that all was well with the world.

MONDAY – JULY 22rd

I treated to breakfast at the hotel as it did not look like a very pleasant morning. We had pancakes and maple syrup. There were German steins and old-fashioned dishes on the wall of the dining room.

We had a flat tire that we noticed before we were ready to start. So we had to wait to have it fixed.

We first had a long detour to the north. The garage man said the new road would be open in about a week – but we didn't wait for it. It rained for a while – long enough for the Star to take on a crust of red mud that stuck closer than a brother throughout the trip.

It soon cleared off, however, and we drove through miles of woods again with here and there a lumber camp.

The Ontanogon River - We crossed many similar ones.

Nearer noon we came into a region of iron mines again. We stopped in Ironwood to have a rattle taken out of the Bendix gear and to get supplies for lunch.

It was a little too early to eat lunch so we drove on. When we crossed the Railroad Tracks we were in Hurley, Wisconsin. Here we saw the first  sign.

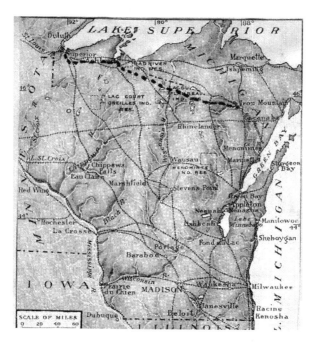

Route Across Wisconsin

    This part of Wisconsin is much like parts of northern Michigan in which the lumber has long been cut off and no other industry has developed to any great extent.

    We drove on and on seeking in vain for a place to eat our lunch. We found no place until we came to Ashland. We ate in the pavilion of the

city park. It was a very hot day by this time, but that was a good place. Had vegetable soup and Philadelphia cream cheese for lunch.

We went through Brule in the afternoon and got into Superior between four and five o'clock.

Then we crossed this Arrowhead Bridge from where we could see them loading boats like this; and when we passed the middle of the bridge, we were in Duluth and in Minnesota.

At Duluth we left US #2 and after a little trouble, we found ‖ *or*

As it was too early to stop for the night we drove on.

We stopped out on a high bluff overlooking the city and took these pictures.

The city below looks like a picture taken from an airplane.

17

A cement pavement stretched away into the distance. We began to look for a place to eat and sleep. The towns are fairly close together, but small, and no one gave a rap for the "tourist".

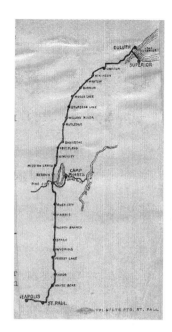

Finally we stopped and cooked and ate supper at Moose Lake. When we were again ready to go it was nine o'clock and dark.

We drove on. The full moon rose — coppery, round, over dark trees. We didn't talk – little towns, no park, no camp, no rooms advertised — perhaps the next one will be the place.

We finally inquired at a filling station. The man said to go on to Pine City. We did. Found the cabin camp after while. All dark and quiet. No one about at all. A dog barked in the filling station, but no one came to the door or answered.

Left there.

Another filling station man directed us to Camp Phares. We finally located it. Mr. Phares in bathrobe and nightcap told us that he had a cottage in which we could stay.

It was midnight — not late at home but very late here, and we were 300 miles from Watersmeet.

Camp Phares

Located on the beautiful shore of Cross Lake and Snake River at Pine City, Minnesota, is an ideal place to spend a vacation or week-end as it is almost midway between the Twin Cities and (Twin Ports) Duluth and Superior.

Camp Phares is just across the lake from Pine City one and a half miles from the center of the village, by road.

The Snake River flows on the north side of the camp and enters into the St. Croix River, which is easily accessible from the camp.

When the mystic night comes stealing
Through my vast green room afar,
Never king had richer ceiling,
Bended bough and yellow star.

- Herbert Bashford

—And a roof over one's head has its advantages, too.

TUESDAY – JULY 23rd

We left Camp Phares at 10:15 after having had breakfast.

St. Paul is a large city, but we did not have any difficulty in finding our way through it. The main street through which we passed was very narrow for the amount of traffic it carried. The buildings flanking it were very tall making the street dark and like a canyon. Down at the end of it is the beautiful St. Paul Cathedral.

We crossed the Mississippi River here. This is a picture of "the Star" on the bridge. The dome standing up above the rest of the city is St. Paul's Cathedral.

This is a picture of the city taken from the bridge.

The valley is flat next to the river and that is used mainly for railroad tracks, then on the next terrace is the business houses, and then still higher up are the residences.

It is St. Paul on the right hand side of the picture, too.

The twin cities are something like this:

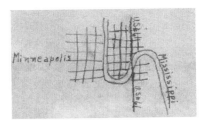

The road was still pavement. In fact it is paved almost to the Iowa line. We went by good farms and small towns. The farming here is diversified: wheat, corn, hay, cattle, etc. All the farmsteads have a grove of large trees, usually willows, around them.

Saw mourning doves. They are not found at home.

We bought some sandwiches and other things about three o'clock and ate them in the car.

We got into Albert Lea between five and six and got a cabin for the night. It was a short driving day but we had come 175 miles and it was good to get settled early. The cabin was small but very conveniently arranged. One bed was on top of the other like bunks of a lumber camp.

I took a shower after supper and the girls did some laundry work; and then we went to bed early quite content and of the opinion that all was well with the world.

WEDNESDAY - JULY 24th

We left Albert Lea at 7:15 and came west on  and US #16 would take us to the park. The telephone poles were also marked with brightly colored bands and AYP (Atlantic, Yellowstone, Pacific Highway) and CBH (Custer Battlefield Highway) so we did not lack for road signs. It was over forty miles to the next town which is named Blue Earth. This is not the land of the filling station and the hot-dog stand, but of farms — the most beautiful farms I have ever seen.

Corn higher, twice and three times higher, than the fences and stretching away farther than eye could see.

Wheat fields. Some in shocks. Some just being cut. Some just ready to be cut. A field of rip-

ened wheat before it is cut, with the wind blowing across it, is a harmony of lights and shadows across bronze.

The farm buildings were large and I did not see an unpainted house or barn all day long. But so many had the hog lot in front of or near the houses. I wish they wouldn't – I wonder why they did.

We ate our dinner at Worthington in a well-kept city park on a lake. It was very warm and we had lima beans for our "piece de resistance" and cold milk for a beverage. It was here that we first met poor water. This did not taste too bad but had a yellow sediment when heated.

We saw more red-headed woodpeckers than any other bird this day. There are no woods such as we have at home, but all the houses have groves around them and there must be many grasshoppers, locusts, etc. as well as grubs.

Between two and three we saw the first South Dakota road sign by which we knew that we had crossed the state boundary line and another state lay behind us.

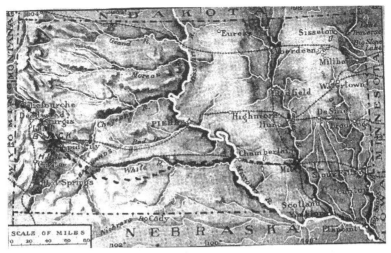

At Brandon, just across the border, we came to a sign which said "road closed on account of high water" and a crudely drawn red arrow pointing vaguely to the left. I drove some two or three miles to the south. There were no signs or directions, and I hesitated.

Along came a car loaded to the brim with family and the papa, seeing our doubt, waved a reassuring hand and sang out "follow me". They had stayed at the same camp we had the night before. Their car bore a South Dakota license plate and they were evidently on familiar ground.

I tried to "follow me" but was barely able to keep his dust in view as I seem physically (or perhaps the trouble is mental) incapable of traveling over forty-five on a strange road. But when we got to Sioux Falls, we got back on our old road again.

We crossed several rivers and they were flooded.

About six o'clock we came to Mitchell. We had traveled 287 miles. We were rather tired when we first got out as the day had been so hot.

We stopped at a large tourist camp and got the last available cottage.

25

We cooked our supper outside to be cooler and then ate inside to get out of the flies.

After supper Mickey and Lucy went after bathing caps in order to take a shower; I got mine first as my hair is indestructible. The shower room was crowded. Here for the first time everyone seemed either to be going to or coming from "the Park".

THURSDAY - JULY 25th

It was hot even when we first got up in the morning and the ants had invaded all our food, at least all that was invadable; but we were soon on our way and a new day's journey was begun.

This part of South Dakota is still like the prairie states – flat or gently rolling – but with fewer trees around the farmsteads and more wheat than any other crop. Miles and miles of wheat.

Horse drawn binders - usually, four, six, or eight horses hitched to them.

More binders were horse drawn than pulled by tractors.

We saw some combines, but not as many as I expected to.

I suppose that they are very expensive.

Most of the grain was still in the field, but we saw many such scenes as this.

.

When we crossed the river, we had to climb up out of the valley again. The country west of the river is much different, much dryer, fewer crops, more grazing cattle. Some on open ranges, or at least the fences were very far apart, and some in smaller lots such as in this picture where they were being fed for marketing, I suppose.

It was very hot, and none of the camping places had any shade; so we bought a lunch at a restaurant. It was a little hot dry dusty town by the name of Murdo. But we felt much more refreshed after our lunch.

Bird life,
as far as numbers are
concerned, was plentiful in
this region. Bobolinks often
flew up from the side of the
road singing and so many of the fence posts
had larks on them.
I never saw so many larks before in my life.
But they were so hot that they sat with
wings out-spread and bills open.

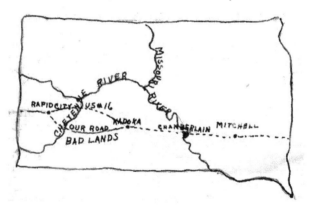

The Bad Lands

And we were
soon in the midst of
them. This picture was
in an old Geography and
it said that the Bad
Lands abounded in dens
of cattle thieves and I
can well see how they
could hide there.

We took this picture soon after we got into the region, as we did not know how much of it there would be, but we need not have been in a hurry as we soon saw much more that was more picturesque than this.

The rocks are a gray cement-like material laid in horizontal layers (must be water deposited) and the layers have not been heaved or buckled by earthquakes.

Then they have been weathered into sharp peaks and unbelievably fantastic shapes.

They seemed to run in ridges with wide plains between them. We crossed a great many dry creek and river beds, the sides of which were nearly perpendicular. I suppose they are full of water in the spring.

The road was narrow, baked hard and full of ruts in places. I don't suppose it would be passable when wet. There was no other traffic.

The map lists four towns on this road but we only saw two. At Interior (I think that whoever named it did so on such a day as the one on which we were there and had in mind the interior of a furnace) we stopped and Mickey bought us some ice cream soda and we consumed much ice water and looked at the fossils, curios, etc. in the store.

We felt better when we went on, but I noticed on

getting in that a rear tire was about worn through, a great stone bruise on it which gave me something to think about when not otherwise occupied.

Scarcely any people live in the region, but once in a while a hut can be seen there where someone has tried to. I don't see why they would think they could, not even grass grows here, only a kind of a moss on the rock.

At Scenic we stopped for gas. The garage man had a little museum in his filling station. He asked us to come in and look at it. It was filled with fossils from the region round about, the most wonderful little stone turtles, mastodon bones, tusks, jaws, and everything, even a fossilized nautilus, and rocks with the imprint of leaves, animal tracks, etc. He said that men from their state University reckoned the age of these things to be between seventy-five and a hundred million years old. He gave me a little deer's jaw bone with teeth in it.

It was forty-seven miles from there out to Rapid City. It soon got dark. We wound down into the Cheyenne River Valley with awful curves and grades. It was too dark to see anything at the side of the road any more. There were trees down here by the river and cicadas making the shrillest loudest noise I ever heard. The road got sandy and almost seemed to end, but didn't quite. None of this road had been marked; we just stayed on it and there was no other to turn off on; but in the dark I could not be sure that there hadn't been. So we just went on. The road got a little better. We saw lights oftener and, finally, about ten o'clock, we got to Rapid City. We had driven 330 miles.

We ate a little supper but did not feel much like it then. I put up the cot, the girls took a shower, and that was another day.

I am glad we saw the Bad Lands.

F R I D A Y - J U L Y 26th

Our cabin faced the south and the sun shone in hot and bright as soon as it was morning; but we were tired and did not get up very early.

Across the road was a fairground. A herd of horses were corralled over there and cowboys looking much like the movie variety were roping them.

There was going to be an Indian encampment here in a few days and they were getting ready.

I drove down town after supplies while the girls got breakfast and I saw Indians coming into town. We saw others when we left the town,  *also. Some rode on horseback, some were in little old wagons in which they had a few camping supplies. Their horses were small and tough looking. Some wore ceremonial dress and others, overalls. The older men wore their hair in braids over each shoulder. The women wore calico dresses and shawls.*

35

We considered turning south and going to the Wind Cave National Park, but decided not to.

We were now approaching the Black Hills. The landscape was becoming more rugged.

We had driven only an hour or so when a tire went flat. While I was jacking the car up, Lucy attempted to take the burs off the bolts that hold the rim. The wrench slipped, she hit her face against the fender and broke the corner of her front tooth. Our first casualty. It was a shame. She had pretty teeth. She felt so bad about it but did not make a fuss. We finished changing the tire and went on to Sturgis which was the next town. There we got a new tire, Mickey bought a new dress and skirt, a dentist put some varnish on Lucy's tooth, we bought a lunch at a restaurant, and started out anew.

We were now in the midst of the Black Hills and although they are called hills, even the atlas classifies them as mountains.

We passed though a small town and started to climb a hill. There was a rough sign at the bottom which said there was a raise of a thousand feet in the next mile. I did not think that the grade could be so steep and foolishly rushed the Star as hard as it would go in high. We went up and up. We came to where a line of cars were parked. People had stopped there at a little spring to put water in their radiators. I stopped, too, and the minute I did the red came up in the motometer and the water in the radiator began to boil like fury. I had to hold the brake and Lucy got out. She said the water was boiling out of it. Of course it was coming out of the overflow pipe, but I couldn't think of that and thought it had blown out a fuse or something. I was far from happy. We let the water out and put fresh water in which was quite a job as the spring only flowed a tiny stream. There after we pursued a slower pace.

We had quite a long stretch of road that was narrow and twisty and unimproved but there was not much traffic through there – though one could not be sure that there wasn't a car around each blind bend until you got around it.

This is a beautiful region. The mountains are heavily timbered with fir – I suppose that is where they get the name "Black" as are the Black Forests of Germany. There are many deep rock canyons, ravines, rapid rivers, and springs. The rock coloring is unique. We passed to the north of Deadwood and south of Belle Fourche where there is a big dam and irrigation project.

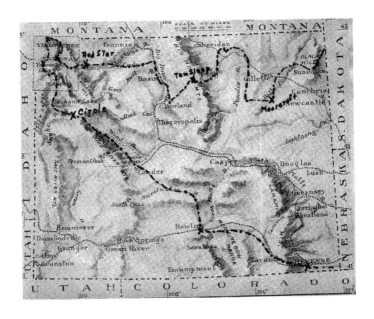

We crossed into Wyoming just before we came to Sundance. The towns in Wyoming have such interesting names. Sundance is one of them, so is Spearfish which is the town in South Dakota at the foot of a big hill.

The Black Hills region extends about sixty miles east and west. While in a very lonely place with no dwelling or no one in sight, just big red mountains all around, the car stopped in that soul sickening way in which the engine just passes away and stepping on the accelerator revives it not at all. There was plenty of gas — the pipe from the vacuum tank to the carburetor was intact — the car was not too hot although we had been climbing and the thermometer at the last filling station had registered 106 degrees. I knew not what to do. A new Ford went past, we hailed. It was a man and his wife and daughter on their way back to California. He was a garage man. He cleaned the carburetor, helped start the engine, kept behind us a while until he was sure we were all right, then swung around us and were again on their way to California. We could see this Devil's Tower when we were over twenty-five

miles from the place where the road turned to go to it. It is eight hundred feet high.

We did not go close to it as it would have been twenty-four miles in to it and back out again, and it was late in the afternoon and we really could see it very well from a distance.

I wonder what forces made it, and when, and why was it left there when the land around it was being worn down.

When we left the Black Hills we came to a level arid region. It had rained a little a short time before we got here and at one time off to our left was a wonderful triple rainbow.

We stopped at Moorcroft for the night. A lady kept the tourist

camp. She lived in the store in the summer and rented her house, woodshed, garage, etc, and some other buildings to travelers. We lived in the sitting room. There was another family in the bedroom and another on the back porch. We had a rocking chair which was a luxury for us.

The water was alkali again as it had been the other side of the mountains.

After supper I took the car down to the garage to have the rod between the lights fixed again. When I came back the girls had my cot all made up and were reading. We soon went to bed and it was another day.

SATURDAY - JULY 27th

The people on the other side of the house started talking about getting up at four and then used the next hour and a half in getting up and getting started. This woke us up and as it was so noisy we couldn't sleep any more, we got up. We had difficulty in getting the cream we had ordered for breakfast but finally succeeded in getting some.

We started out that morning in a region of sagebrush plains, but it was not long before we could see hills in front of us. They were scattered about the landscape. We did not have to climb them, we went around them. But we no sooner got around some than others loomed up ahead of us.

Settlements are very far apart and very small here. In fact we went through Wild Cat without seeing it; and we were really looking for it, too, as it has such an interesting name.

We stopped at Spotted Horse for gas and oil. The village consisted of a combined store, filling station, and garage, one house, and a schoolhouse. The population consists of one family. The man was glad to see us, I think. He was brought up in Michigan on a farm near Sand Lake and liked to talk about Michigan; but he said that he "would never come back to Michigan to live'" as it was easier to earn a living here. But it was such a vacant place. I should have thought he would have liked more companionship. The winters must be like the one described in Giants in the Earth.

After we left Spotted Horse Lucy first noticed snow-capped mountains. We wondered how far away they were and determined to find out by watching the speedometer. It was seventy-five miles or more. Imagine seeing from here to the Straits of Mackinaw or from here to Alpena.

These are the Big Horn Mountains. We watched them all morning. Sometimes it seemed that we were going to pass to the north of them, sometimes to the south — that is if we ever got to them at all. We passed around one chain of foothills after another but always the snow-caps were ahead of us.

Sometimes we lost sight of the peaks we had watched for miles and got sight of others as the road wound about through the hills and across wide plains between.

We stopped and cooked and ate our lunch at Buffalo.

The road made a turn in the town and we were no sooner out of town than we were in the mountains. And the Big Horns are mountains. Most of the driving had to be in second, but the Star pulled up easily and quietly withal and slowly.

Much of the region on the eastern slope of the mountains is a national forest reserve. It is timbered with lodge pole pine. In the openings we saw a great many herds of Hereford cattle and we liked to try to read the brands on them.

In the afternoon we stopped at the Elk Horn Hunting Lodge and had a cold drink. It was a kind of a club house I believe although there was no one there at that time except some people who worked there. The rooms — we were in the dining room and sitting room — were very large. The furnishings were rustic but ample. The fireplaces were immense and a great many hunting and fishing trophies were about. The porch railings were made of elk horns. Elk live in these mountains and like other members of the deer family they drop their horns every year. Probably that is how the Big Horns got their name.

We continued to climb and climb. We were not among the snow fields, but surely we must be nearing the tip. We had long ago ceased to try to keep any one peak in view because we twisted and turned so.

We had just broke over the top and commenced to go down when we met a car. The place was narrow, I had the inside, I got over as far as possible and pinched the inside rear tire against the cliff that rose perpendicularly from the road. It went flat. I held on to the brakes while the girls blocked the wheels, then I got out and we blocked it some more for the whole landscape slanted down at a terrific pitch.

We jacked it up and I had just discovered that the jack would not lift it far enough to enable us to take the tire off and get the other on. Also there was one burr that I could not turn, try as I might. Then a Model T Ford roadster drove around us and stopped. And a man asked us it we wanted help. We did. He got his jack, lifted the car higher, put on the other tire, and pumped more air into it by hand as he did not think there was air enough in it.

He was charming — if I know the meaning of the word. He told us that in 1876 when he was nine years old he and his father built the first house in Rapid City and that the Indians had them penned in for two weeks. He said he had a niece, who was a school teacher, who had visited him and liked the mountains. I do not think that he had other relatives. He must have been over sixty but he did not seem that old. He told us that it was about twenty miles on to Ten Sleep, which was the next town, and that the grades were very steep. He asked me if I were afraid to drive in mountains and I said I wasn't when I went slowly. He said that sometimes men who had not driven mountains before were shaking with nervousness when they got to Ten Sleep and were unable to eat or sleep.

When the tire was changed I went ahead, but he soon passed us. The steepness and the curves were the worst that I ever saw. To look  down to the river at the bottom of the canyon was sickening. My chest ached from holding my breath so much but I didn't know it until afterwards.

Twice "our friend" as we called him, and meant it, waited for us at the foot of dangerous places to see if we were all right and our tires were whole.

He didn't speak to us — just looked us over and went on.

45

We finally got down on a level with the river and began to breathe freely again when the mountains began to close in on us which was even worse. I

had rather be on top and look on into eternity than to be at the bottom and have the rocks crowd me so. I actually felt crushed, as if they were so close that there was not room enough to breathe.

But that wasn't such a long stretch. The bare rocks gave way to wooded slopes again. Our friend was waiting for us where the road turns off in the picture. He was going to turn off there he said. He asked us if we wouldn't like a nice room and an opportunity to have a warm bath; and if we did, here was a widow lady who was a little off the line of travel and did not get many tourists who would be glad to have us. So evidently we were not the only one to whom he intended to do a good turn to that day.

We drove on to Ten Sleep - which certainly belongs in the list of towns that have unusual names along with Spearfish, Sundance, Spotted Horse, Wild Cat, Crazy Woman, etc. A man told us that the Shoshones and the Crows used to hold meetings on the river, and that it was "ten sleeps" or ten days journey between reservations and that the white man had taken the name of the river for the town and shortened it to Ten Sleep.

The cabins were all full when we got there, but we did get a double room from the "widow lady". No bed to make, clean sheets and pillow cases, rocking chair, warm water - luxuries.

TEN SLEEP INN
Ten Sleep, Wyoming

We went to The Inn for dinner. The food was served in big dishes and when one was empty it was filled – and one stayed there until he was satisfied. Food was sure good, too. It was more like a family gathering than like a hotel. At the table with us were a family from Escanaba. We looked like folks from home to each other. They had been to the Park and told us a lot about it.

It was late when we got through eating, not due entirely to the fact that we ate a lot, but we had started late. Then we went to get the tire that was being fixed and to buy some food for Sunday. By this time the town (population one hundred) was filled with cowboys and their horses. There were no sidewalks and the horses were parked all over the place where most towns have walks. The men wearing big hats and high heeled boots whooped and yelled. Very interesting, withal, but we turned in quite early - it had been a large day.

I have no picture of the Brown Hotel. I wish I had.

SUNDAY - JULY 28th

We left Ten Sleep quite early in the morning and set out in search of a church as there is none in that town. The region west of Ten Sleep is called the Painted Badlands. The formation is similar to that of "the land that God forgot" in South Dakota but the peaks and ridges are not in such fantastic shapes. But in places the coloring is lovely — reds, yellow, mauves and lavender.

We saw hundreds of prairie dogs. Mickey tried several times to get a picture, but I could not seem to stop at the right time and place. They would sit up so straight and still while we were watching them, but when we would take our eye off them to get the camera ready, they would disappear - sort of like the leprechaun or fairy shoemaker in the Irish folk story.

It was about thirty miles to Worland, the first town. We stopped there, but they only had church every other Sunday and this was the other Sunday.

We turned north here along the Big Horn River. This is an irrigated valley and they raise a lot of alfalfa. Some thirty miles farther we came to Basin. We found a small church but there was no one there. Probably we were too late. We tried to eat here, but they did not want to serve us at the hotel. It was too late for breakfast and too early for noon. So we went on to Greybull. Mickey bought the dinner and while the girls were ordering I took the car to the garage to have the brakes tightened.

Then we went on over scorching hot sagebrush plains to Cody. At

the end of the main street and a little way out is this statue of Buffalo Bill. It was sculpted by Gertrude Vanderbilt Whitney. There is a museum of his things, too, but we did not go in. We drove by it and saw an old stage coach which was out in front. Some way I had always thought of them as being something like a closed car inside, but they are <u>so little</u>.

We had not left Cody long before we were on what is probably one of the most scenic drives in United States - the Cody road.

We were driving up Sulfur Creek. We saw geyser craters and smelled sulfur.

The creek joins the Shoshone River. This bridge in the picture is Hayden bridge. This is the region of Owen Wister's novel the Virginian - referred to in that book at least as Stinking Water.

The land grew rougher, the road steeper, the river swifter, the road narrower, the mountains still higher, the road still steeper, and more and more and more.

We did not know what was coming. In fact all the geography that we knew about this region all together was not much, but we know more now and that was a good way to learn it.

Road in Shoshone Canyon
Looking toward Cody
F.J. Hiscock Photo-Cody

The arrow shows the way we were going. This is a picture of the mountains getting higher, the river getting swifter, and the road getting steeper and narrower.

Due to a turn in the road, you can not see through the tunnel (left hand side of the picture) and it is impossible to pass a car when in there. I honked the horn, drew a deep breath, and went in. It is not so very long - fortunately.

This is a picture of the mountains getting *still higher*. Imagine a man planning a road through such a place - and then *putting* one there. I don't think there will ever be many women road-builders.

I never could be, I know, I never could have imagined this road before it was done.

"The Dam Hill"
Shoshone Canyon
F.J. Hiscock
Cody, Wyo.

The first tunnel (the same one that is in the pre-ceding picture) is in the lower right hand corner of this picture.

This picture shows the steepness of the road, too. It had to be climbed in low.

This shows the dam, too.

"The Shoshone Gorge" FJ Hiscock Photo

This shows the steepness of the road still better. See the road in the lower right hand corner, you lose sight of it in the picture; but it is several flights of stairs above the top of the dam, and the top of the dam is some two hundred feet above the river.

This picture shows the foam and spray from the water in the spillway better, too.

Shoshone Dam
and Spillway.
F.J.Hiscock Photo

This shows the road above the top of the dam. Also how the spillway comes through the rock and the steps, which are little more than ladders, down which the workmen climb to get to the bottom of the dam. Only employees can use them - I don't know as I would feel a need for going down anyway. The spillway is 300 feet long.

Road Tunnel and Spillway
Shoshone Reservoir.
FJ Hiscock. Photo - Cody

The "x" is not where the body was found but where we parked the car. The white water is where the spillway begins. The dam is the other side of the tunnel.

A great many people were there the same time we were.

We watched the water from over the railing a little while and then walked though the tunnel back to see the dam.

Top of Shoshone Dam and Reservoir. F Hiscock Photo Cody, Wyo

The car was on the other side of the tunnel in the picture.

The building between the two flights of steps from the road is really as big as a little house. The top of the dam is ten feet wide, even at that I wanted to hold on to the railing in going down the stairs and <u>did</u> out on the top of the dam, but the feeling wore off after a little. Perhaps some of it was due to the high altitude, but probably most of it was due to a fear of high places and to the fact that I don't breathe much when driving in such a place. I wonder why.

Shoshone Dam as seen
from an Airplane.
F J Hiscock Photo Cody Wyo.

The dam backs up the water into reservoir or
Shoshone Lake which is some ten miles long, an average
width of four miles, and is some two hundred feet deep.

As can be seen in the picture, the rock reaches
out into the lake in points and there are tunnels through
these places so that the road can get through, as it cannot
get around.

Tourist Cars on Cody-Yellowstone
Highway. Shoshone Canyon.
FJ Hiscock-Photo-Cody, Wyo.

    This is another view of the road west of the dam along the reservoir.

    The car in the foreground is one of the big yellow buses from the park. They have five seats and three people on each seat. The top is down so that they can see up and down better, a thing that you cannot do in a closed car. But don't ladies get sunburned in them! And how funny they look with masks of paper napkins, etc. in trying to prevent it.

This is a series of three tunnels, the third one is a little longer than the other two but not much; the road curve is why you cannot see through it in the picture.

We also saw the Chinese wall, a queer zig zag formation of rock extending north and south.

The road leads us through Shoshone National Forest, too. It has a colossal entrance. There is a high mountain on each side of the river, each one has a high peak and on both of them there is a flag pole and a flag flying.

In one place there is a rock over the road that looks like a laughing pig.

To the south in one place there was a great jumble of rocks that is called " the garden of the goops ".

The Holy City.
© 1922 by F.J.Hiscock.
Cody, Wyo.

From across the river and at a distance these rocks look like an eastern city with towers and temples and minarets.

Among these rocks there is one that looks like a goose, another like an anvil, and one like a wooden shoe.

Just beyond here the river makes a triple bend which is known as " the Devil's elbow ". We crossed the river here on a narrow bridge.

When we crossed again a few miles farther on there was a rock against the sky-line to the left that looked like four old men sliding down hill in a toboggan.

Then for some distance along the river there was a palisade formation and the road was narrow and close to the river again.

The sun was getting low enough so that it shone in our eyes and that made it hard to drive so we wanted a place to stay.

"Chimney Rock"

We passed this rock. I wonder how it came to be that shape.

Finally we came to the Red Star camp. It was back away from the road some distance. As all this is a national forest there are no billboards or advertising signs; there was just a small sign where the road turned in. I like that.

We rented the tent (frame walls and floor) across the little creek. We were the "poorer class of people who live across the river" this night.

There was a store and several cabins to this camp. The lady was nice. The man was queer. Mickey said he had had a stroke.

The view of the mountains from our doorway was wonderful. I liked the sound of the creek just outside the bedroom wall, too.

We had a flat tire when we got there. LeRoy from Ohio changed it for us while supper was cooking.

We were just four miles from the Park.

(See map on following page)

Yellowstone

National

Park

1929

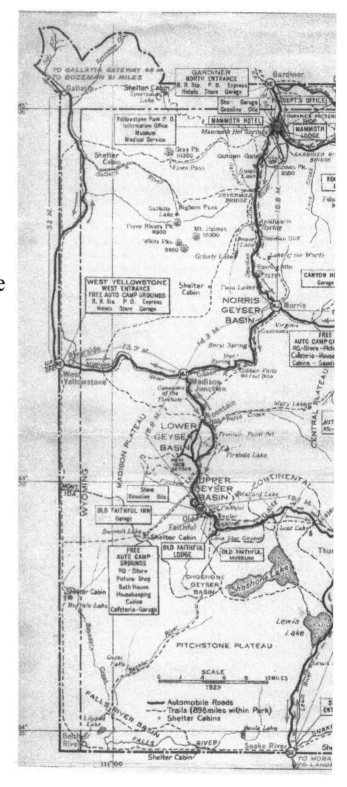

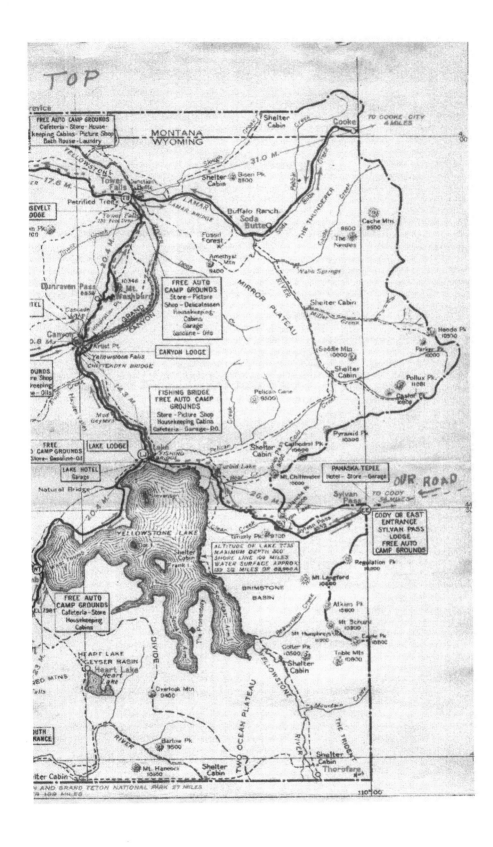

It had been very cold during the night and Lucy had had a nervous chill or an attack of indigestion or combination of them. But the morning was bright and sunshiny and there was wood enough so that we got breakfast on the little wood stove, so that we soon got warmed up and ready to start.

We stopped at a garage and had one tire fixed and bought a new one, discarding the one that was stone-bruised so badly. That took quite a long time, but when it was done we were soon at <u>THE PARK.</u> We were 2038 miles from home. We paid the ranger three dollars; he gave us our permit, a guide to the park, and marked out our route on leaving in the split part of a minute, and waved us on our way. I felt some like sitting a few minutes in order to more fully realize that we were really here, but the cars behind wanted our place. So we went on to see what we should see.

There is a camp and ranger station just inside the gates but we had nothing to stop there for. The road from here to Yellowstone Lake is known as Sylvan Pass. It is very mountainous. It is heavily wooded mostly with lodge-pole pine, but some spruce and fir. As this is an entrance and an exit to the park, cars go both ways on it. In places it is too narrow for cars to a pass. It is very crooked, too, so it is often impossible to see a car coming. On curves there are signs telling you to sound your horn and proceed slowly. I always did but I always wondered if the other driver wouldn't be so busy sounding his horn that he would not hear mine. But I went slowly — so very.

They are building the road wider I think as we passed several camps of road workers. Leroy told us the *evening before that they closed the gate at six o'clock and worked on the road at night.*

When we were up — high up on a ledge like a shelf on the side of the moun-tain, — the car just ahead of us, and the one coming from the other way, could not pass so cross-section *they stopped and everyone behind each of them had to. The car coming east was a large coupe and in it was a man and his wife from Illinois. She was quite an old lady; but in an instant she was out of the car, made the car ahead of us move about six inches back and then about a foot ahead - al-though I think the driver was in a funk as she had to insist that he do it. Then she moved her husband a little bit — he moved the way she told him, too, then moved the other man a little again, motioned to me to stay where I was — I never intended to move until she told me to anyway — and her husband got around to where the road was wider, and all the cars going east that were too close to the edge for com-fort, moved on and the jam was over. She surely knew how to do it, but she was so sarcastic that I think most everyone felt like biting her before we got out of there.*

This road is part of Sylvan Pass. It is called the Corkscrew Drive. I have heard of roads so crooked that they cross themselves, but this one actually does. I won-der if there is any other like it in the world.

The steep grades do not show in the picture, but they are very steep. The Star had to take part of it in low. In fact, the road is a device for getting vehicles up a great distance in just a short way. There was snow near the road here and the mountains looked very forbidding.

Sylvan Lake and
Thunder Mountain
F.J. Hiscock-Cody

We passed two lakes on this road. This one is Sylvan Lake and it is very pretty. The other one is Turbid Lake. It is muddy due to springs on the bottom. There were Mallard ducks on it close to shore.

I thought that this nest might be an eagle's nest even though I knew that they build their nests on crags of rock, for it is so large, and the

young bird that stuck his head over the edge of the nest and made such a babyish noise for one so big, was dark with a white head. But it is an osprey's nest. An osprey is a big fish hawk. They usually build their nests in the crags of a canyon. They mate for life and use the same nest over again. The next day we saw one swoop down several hundred feet into the swirling water below, come up with a fish, rise, pause in mid-air, shake himself like a dog to rid his feathers of water, and take the fish to his nest.

About twenty-six miles from the entrance we came to Yellowstone Lake Station. These stations or junctions are much alike. There you will find a hotel, lodge, garage, filling station, general store, cafeteria or delicatessen, picture shop, auto camp, and housekeeping cabins.

We ate our lunch in the auto camp. There are so many trees, and water, and everything is so convenient, and it is so clean that it is delightful. Here we first made the acquaintance of the bears.

There are hundreds of bears in the park. The black bears roam about all over and get their food from garbage cans and from what people throw them.

They are quite accustomed to being photographed and fed by man, but they are still wild animals. The park

rules forbid people to feed them, but most everyone does; sometimes they are bitten in doing so, but as a ranger said that in taking a census of all those who had been, none had ever been bitten twice.

Some are black and some are a cinnamon brown. The brown is just a color phase of the black bear family as black mothers often have brown cubs and vice versa.

This fellow went around knocking over garbage cans — just for fun, because he wasn't hungry, for he wouldn't eat the food that was thrown to him. An employee would yell at him and brandish a stick at him, and if that did no good, he picked up the garbage can.

In the picture he is reaching for some candy held by a big little boy who delighted to demonstrate his way with bears to timid ladies who wanted to take pictures of bears.

Some bears have learned how to get into cars. Some people coax in order to get their picture there. And sometimes they learn by smelling food in a car and stealing it out and thereby get the idea that all cars carry bacon under the back seat. We saw a bear climb up on to the top of a closed car. Two woman were in the car. They were very miserable; they did not want to be where they were, and they most certainly did not want to move.

There is something about a black bear that is like a clown. I don't know whether it is his facial expression or the way he does things.

Their walk is different than any other four-footed animal that I know. Their two right feet go ahead at the same time, and then their two left feet, with their head swinging between their shoulders.

After we had the dishes washed and things packed into the car again (we had potato salad for lunch which was quite unusual as it seemed well nigh unto impossible to boil more potatoes at night than we would eat), we went to see the Lake which is much lower than the camp grounds. It is very large and very blue. The guide book says that it covers 139 square miles and has a shore line of a hundred miles. It is sandy for some distance back from the shore. Probably at one time the lake was much larger — during the time of glaciers — perhaps.

When we left Lake Junction we went out across this Fishing Bridge. It was filled with fishermen, some of whom had some beautiful trout. All the streams and lakes are open to fishing here and one is allowed to catch ten in one day.

A short distance beyond here where the road is near the lake we saw a couple of pelicans and a little farther a swan swimming in the water — I never thought I would see one — a wild one. They are just as graceful as their pictures - even more so.

Some five or six miles from Lake Junction we came to the mud geysers. They are great pits in which gray-greasy mud bubbles and thumps like thick porridge. The earth and the paths between them is gray and hard like baked clay. They have the disagreeable smell of sulfur.

The last one we looked at is called The Dragon's Mouth. It is in sort of a cave in a side hill and is more liquid than some of the others. It glubbles a while and then shoots out a lot of steam and hot water that smells like a laundry washing very dirty clothes.

Seven or eight miles farther on we came to the Chittenden Bridge. We took the right hand turn, went down the road a ways, parked the car, and got out and looked at the Upper Falls.

Up until this time they are the largest falls I had ever seen. For scenery I like mountains and waterfalls better than any-thing else.

These are over a hundred feet high, such a roar, such a mist, rainbows where the sun shines on it.

We were on the side where I have marked a "x", only farther toward the fore-ground.

After watching the water a while we followed a trail that led down near the river then a stiff climb up out of the canyon again.

We came out in back of the Lodge. On the way back to the car we saw a young black bear up in a tree like this.

We drove back to the bridge, took the other turn up past the stores, etc. and rented us a cabin for the night. It had a wooden floor and half sides; the rest of the walls were awning and the roof canvas.

It was quite early when we got our beds made and supper started. I lay down on the bed and fell asleep. When I awoke it was dark. I thought that they either must have eaten without me or were waiting for me to wake up. I asked them why they hadn't called me, at which they both wailed that the potatoes had been boiling for <u>three hours</u> and were <u>still hard</u>. That was our first experience in boiling things in a high altitude.

But they were soon done after that and we ate them with canned spinach by the light of one flickering candle, and they sure tasted good. I <u>liked</u> the spinach although I usually feel like the Irishman who said "he was glad he didn't like it, for if he liked it he would probably eat some of it and he hated the darned stuff". We had fat little wieners, too, but Lucy regarded the spinach as a fine idea. She is a <u>very</u> good cook and paid attention that we had a balanced ration including vitamins, minerals, roughage, etc, and she had been concerned over our lack of green stuff over the arid plains. Mickey had suggested that we get out and graze on some alfalfa, but we had not quite reached that stage yet.

We went to bed after we had the dishes done. We could hear the roar of the falls when the camp was quiet for the night.

It had been a large day.

T U E S D A Y - J U L Y 30th

The night was cold. When we got up in the morning and went after water there was a big black bear on the doorstep. (If in doubt as to whether this

was our doorstep, note our little gasoline can on the doorstep.)

This is the same bear out in the sunshine and it is a plainer picture.

This picture partly shows how the housekeeping cabins were arranged in streets much like a city. There are some three or four hundred of them here. Mammoth Hot Springs and Old Faithful camps are larger.

After breakfast and we had things packed in, we set out to see the Canyon and the Falls.

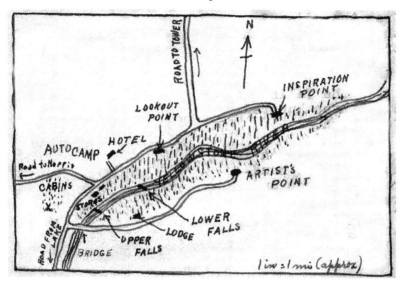

This is a sort of map of the region.

First we went back to the bridge, crossed it, and went to Artist's Point. It was from here that Moran painted the picture of the falls that hangs in the capitol building at Washington. There is a platform out over the canyon so that you can see the falls and the canyon. There were many people there but no one talked and if any of them belonged to each other they stayed close together. It is so big that it makes you feel lonely. One thinks when you first look at it that you will look and look — but you can't, if it is the first time you have seen it. You must get away, see something familiar, get your familiar backgrounds and attitudes back, get in touch with something human, or you can't stand the feelings that it gives you.

This is taken from the side of the platform on the trail.

The falls are over three hundred feet high.

The canyon is about twelve hundred feet deep and two thousand feet from one side to another.

Then we went back to the bridge again, out past the

stores and along the north edge of the canyon.

There was a mother bear with twin cubs in the road. It was good to watch and think about something alive and funny and young and little.

On the north side of the canyon there are steps leading down to the foot of the falls. This picture was taken here.

We parked the car and walked out on to the edge of the canyon. This was at Point Lookout.

Here was a forest ranger and some tourists. His explanations and conversation helped to take some of the awfulness away.

Here we saw many osprey nests on the tops of crags below.

The coloring of the rocks in the canyon is marvelous. Every shade of yellow is there, many oranges, and here and there a splash of red. Evergreen trees growing here and there in the crevices of the rocks further add to the color harmony.

The mineral in the rocks is a kind of iron oxide (limonite). At one time hot springs fumes came up through the rock and disintegrated it causing these colors.

The canyon is some twenty miles long, but only these first three are colored.

When we got into the car again we drove to the fork in the road and took the right hand fork to Inspiration Point. These pictures are from that point. The *platform on the right hand side of the upper picture is Point Lookout.*

This road into Inspiration Point is level and in the midst of a Lodge-pole pine forest. In one place just to the left of the road is a glacier boulder half as large as our house. It has no angular edges, it is all smoothed off, there are still some grooves along the side of it. According to its formation it must have been carried at least twenty miles.

After being at Inspiration Point we drove back to the last fork in the road and took the road to Tower Falls.

If ever I go to the Park again I think I would like to stay at the Canyon longer. It is the best part of the park to me. The geyser, the hot springs, and the climb up Mount Washburn come next.

We had gone only a few miles when we began to climb. The weather by this time was very hot. When we had ascended some two or three miles, we came to a long line of cars that had stopped to cool off their engines and fill up with water. There was water there and a sign that said that it was the last water until you were through Dunraven Pass.

There were girls in the car ahead of us. They took a hot water bottle to get water to pour into the radiator. We thought that was funny. That morning the people across the street had given us a chunk of ice and I had broken it up and put it in the water jug, so we did not want to take the jug to get water for our radiator. So Lucy took the coffee pot and the girls in the car ahead thought that was a funny thing to use – and it was.

A couple of cars ahead was a Texan in a new Ford. He was just about a nervous wreck over the climb. As he got out of his car he mopped the perspiration from off his fevered brow and cursed his car because it would not pull.

This had been one of those places in which the whole land-scape had slanted upward. It was impossible to tell with the eye that there was any grade at all and hard to believe that there was such a steep one. This was evidently the first time he had ever encountered such a place and he was worried over his engine — thought that it had no power. He felt some better when everyone told him that they had been driving in second most of the time for several miles back.

A short distance farther we came to a fork in the road. One led through Dunraven Pass and the other over Mount Washburn. Both came out the same place and the one through the pass is shorter and the grades are easier — we took the other.

Soon the Star could no longer go in second and we went into low. The road was only one car wide — here is one place that "having put your hand to the plow" you can't turn back — there is no place in which to turn around. I wouldn't have any way — but I thought a little bit about what would happen if something went wrong with the car; then I wouldn't let myself any more. Up and up, it was so steep that the front of the car looked queer, we stood at such an unusual angle. The curves were short and close together. Sometimes there were wider places on the curves where one could stop and look down on the country below. We stopped once or twice. I did not want to after that. Driving in low so long does something to me as a driver. I keep thinking about my lack of reserve power. But the Star climbed steadily and coolly up and up.

As we got up higher the sides of the mountain be-came one vast flower garden. Made me think of the de-scription of the flowers on the sides of the Alps in Heidi.

They were all very small, but so many kinds and colors, and so fragrant that we could smell them even in the car.

Sometimes we could get a glimpse of the top on which there was a flag flying, but it was so high above us that it was not a comfort to look for it. But after about four miles of this (it seemed much farther), we commenced to wind about the top in a spiral and after making several turns we burst out onto the top.

There is a little rock house on the top and the flag flies from the top of it. There were three or four cars already parked up there, and there was room for several more although the top is relatively small.

We could look out into miles and miles of space. Just mountains and forests and lakes and sky.

I think I know why ancient peoples worshipped in high places.

This is the road up. The road seen in the foreground is one of the last spirals.

This is the road down. It goes down the other side of the mountain. The patch of white is a snow field as big as three city blocks. Note the curves in the road.

I am glad we climbed Mount Washburn.

It was after noon when we left and we had to go down slowly (ten miles an hour in low) as the grades are so steep.

We had our lunch in the automobile camp at Tower Junction. There were many funny little pack rats that scampered over the ground from table to table and ate the crumbs.

It was then between two and three o'clock but it is less than eighteen miles on to Mammoth Hot Springs. So we packed up the lunch box and went on.

Our first stop was to see Tower Falls. We parked the car down below by the river and climbed up the trail.

These are very pretty falls. I liked them. A load of people from the yellow busses were there. Some could not see them at all after having seen the falls of the Yellowstone. They were hot and tired and

cross. They would have liked them if they had been in Iowa. It is easy to lose one's perspective if you look at the Park too fast.

The water drops over one hundred thirty feet over the rocks here. The name Tower comes from the formation of the rock in this region. It is worn in sharp towers and minarets.

Across the top of a mountain on the other side of the river there is a layer of rock that looks like a breastwork of a fort, that is like the stockades around the old colonial blockhouses. I think it is a layer of lava that for some reason cooled quickly and so formed into six-sided columns.

On leaving here we passed by a cliff of basalt (I think) in columnar form that overhung the road. A little farther on we saw what is called the Needle. It is a spire of rock that rises from the bed of the river up some three hundred feet.

A little farther on we turned off the Loop Road and drove about three-quarters of a mile to see a petrified tree.

There is a petrified forest about seven miles from here, but you have to go on horseback and take a guide — we hadn't the money.

About ten miles farther on in a mountain meadow we saw a beaver dam and house on Lava Creek.

We crossed a long bridge over the Gardiner River and were then soon at Mammoth Hot Springs camp.

We got a cabin for the night. We decided to stay over all the next day to see what we should see, get some extra rest which we were beginning to feel the need of, and do some laundry work, which we were also sadly in need of.

After supper we went to the laundry, rented a washboard, and two of us washed while the other one took a shower. We took turns at this until everything and everybody was clean. Then Mickey and I had a wild time putting up the clothes line and getting the clothes hung out to dry.

We got to bed quite early and decided to go with the ranger when he took a party around to see the hot spring at eight-thirty in the morning as it would be enjoyable and good for us to walk.

WEDNESDAY - JULY 31st

Most of our clothes were dry and ready to take down. After breakfast we did the dishes and then drove the car to Liberty Cap. Parked it near there and waited for the forest ranger to come to conduct the people over the hot springs formations. There were some thirty or forty people that started out when he came – not that many were present when we were officially dismissed, however. Many must have perished by the wayside.

Liberty Cap is an extinct hot spring cone. It stands about forty feet high and is shaped like the mob caps worn at the time of the French Revolution. It is made of gray calcium carbonate or travertine, as is all the hot spring formation of the region and has been left standing like that due to processes of erosion.

The underlying rock of all of Capitol Hill is travertine, but soil had been hauled onto it to make lawns around the buildings.

This is a sort of a map of this part of the park. This is where the fort was and all the soldiers quartered when the parks were under the control of the War Department of the government.

The Superintendent's office is here, the post office, museum, weather bureau, hospital, rangers' homes, etc.

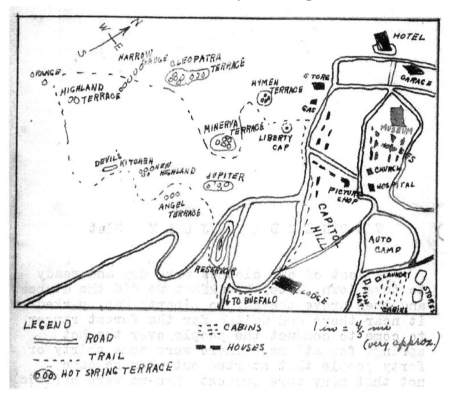

Our hike started at Liberty Cap. First we circled around Hymen Terrace which is no longer active. The terraces were cold and gray and dry. The travertine is hard like cement, but we were told to keep on the trail as there are places where it will not hold up.

From there the trail led to Minerva Terrace. This is active and very beautiful. The water is not boiling, but hot, about 180 degrees. As it comes up out of the

ground it has calcium carbonate dissolved in it. As the water cools the mineral drops out of solution and is deposited. It is deposited more on the outside edges and that is why terraces are built up.

The colors are due to algae that live in the hot water. They are mostly shades of orange, yellow and brown, but one was almost entirely made up of shades of blue.

87

When a spring is no longer active the algae die and there is no color left, just the gray travertine terraces.

Then the trail bears to the right past Cleopatra Terrace and then up a flight of stairs out on to a ridge which was built up by a spring.

Then the trail leads up over the Narrow Gauge Spring (see picture, also map).

The water issues out of a long narrow slit in the ground. The ranger stood on top and gave each one a hand up so that one stood on it and could see along it and down into it better.

By this time it had started to rain. I had guessed wrong and left my raincoat in the car.

From here the trail was more wooded, mountain cedars and Engelman spruce, but they are stunted and twisted and torn by the winds of winter.

At Orange Spring Mound we waited for a group of people who were going over the Nature Trail. When they got there we went on to the Devil's Kitchen.

On the way we saw a mule-eared deer with twin fawns still in their dappled coats.

The Devil's Kitchen is an ancient hot spring fissure. We went down into it. It is narrow and deep and dark. Bats hang upside down in it.

Up to this time we had been climbing, now we began to descend—which is quite as hard on the leg muscles.

This is New Highland Terrace. It is one of the most attractive due to its mound shape and unique coloring.

Then we went by Angel Terrace which used to be active, but wasn't when we were there.

These springs vary often, one drying up and another breaking forth.

Angel terraces are snowy white. There are stubs of dead trees imbedded in the travertine.

Then we came past the hot spring where the algae is so blue.

Then we came to Jupiter, probably the greatest hot spring in the world, marvelous for its size, coloring, and the beauty of its formation. It is Jupiter that we saw steaming from our cabin in the sunset the evening before.

Here the ranger left us. And the girls and I and a few others went down past the reservoir to the buffalo corral.

There are nearly a thousand buffalo in the park,

but as they are dangerous animals they are kept up on the Lamar River away to the northwest and to get there you have to go on horseback.

So in the summer time they keep some fifteen or twenty of them in a corral here.

We saw an elk when we went to see the buffalo.

Then we went to where the car was parked and went to our cabin.

We had walked over three miles and had lifted ourselves up over four hundred feet and then lowered ourselves the same distance.

In the afternoon we all slept a while. Then

we went to the museum. There we saw many interesting things, stuffed specimens of the rarer animals of the park, also birds, fossils, a rock on which there were prints of leaves (they looked like chestnut leaves; and there are *no deciduous trees in this region at all now except a few cottonwoods on some of the river bottoms), relief maps of the park (I was wishing to see one), also ... a geological man, pictures of people who first explored the park, labeled rock specimens, labeled flower specimens and many other things.*

We visited the Curio Shop. I bought a little knife for Mother to keep on the sitting room table for opening letters, etc, wished vainly for more money to spend.

Late in the afternoon the girls took the laundry to the room back of the delicatessen, rented an iron and ironed them, while I got the supper. I started early so as to give the potatoes time to boil. Cooked mashed potatoes, peas, hamburg and tea all on two burners. Supper was ready when they came back; so that was done.

After dark we went over to the Auto Camp where they had a bon-fire and listened to a lecture by a ranger. It was a good talk.

After that we dressed for a cold night and went to bed.

THURSDAY - AUGUST 1st

We left Mammoth in the morning. The clouds were lower than the top of Mt. Evart. As we were leaving they were just floating away.

A few miles from Mammoth we went by the Silver Gate and the Hoodoos. In this place are several acres on which are piled great blocks of travertine, helter skelter, here and there. They were probably knocked down there from some higher place by an earthquake shock. Perhaps they were scraped off by a glacier, but I don't think there was a glacier here after the hot springs started.

A little farther on we came to the Golden Gate, where the road goes over a viaduct. Must have been a difficult bit of engineering, building this road.

At the head of this canyon is Rustic Falls. They are pretty falls, dropping about sixty or seventy feet.

As soon as the falls are passed the road drops quickly down into a mountain valley called Swan Lake Flat.

Mountain peaks of the Galletin Range can be seen on the right. We

passed Swan Lake, and a couple of miles farther we crossed the Gardiner River. Here we entered Willow Park. We hoped we would see a moose here, but we didn't; I think it was too late in the morning.

Then we came to Apollinaris Spring. Two flights of stone steps lead up to it. The water has some kind of dissolved mineral in it.

Next we came to Obsidian Cliff. This is made of black volcanic glass.

It is said that Jim Bridger when he returned to Missouri after his sojourns in the west told such tall stories that his neighbors did not believe him; so he made his accounts larger and larger. One of his stories was something like this:

"One day I was hunting. I saw an elk not far away and pulled up and shot at him. He did not even raise his head, but kept on eating grass. I fired again — and nothing happened. This made me so mad that I ran up to him to club him in the head with my gun — and I smashed my gun on a mountain of clear glass. The elk was ten miles away on the other side of the mountain. It was really only a fawn anyway as the clear glass mountain had also acted as a magnifying glass."

The road was built along the side of it by making fires along it; and then when the rock was hot, by dashing cold water on them causing the rock to splinter. The Indians used the same method to get sharp splinters of rock for their arrows, although on the whole they avoided the park as they were in superstitious fear of its phenomena.

On the right of Obsidian Cliff is Beaver Lake. There is a beaver dam there, but it looks very old.

Next we came to Roaring Mountain (picture on next page). Just looking at it gave me a weird scary

feeling. It is said that twenty-five years ago there was just one steam vent on the very top of the mountain and that since then more have burst forth every year. The trees between there and the road are all killed and stand there as dead stubs.

Then we passed two small lakes. There is a stream flowing between them, but one is green and the other blue — I wonder why.

Bijah Spring is near the road.

The Frying Pan is a hot spring that stews away like grease in a skillet.

Then we crossed the Gibbon River and came to the Norris Ranger Station. There is an auto camp there, but no stores.

Here we took the right hand road and were soon at Norris Geyser Basin.

95

We parked above and to the left of this picture and came down this path. They call the rock around these geysers geyserites. I think a geologist if he found the same kind of rock somewhere else, he would call it siliceous sinter. There is a board walk out over it (middle of picture) as it is not safe to walk on. There are several geysers out here (one can be seen in the picture) some are just quiet pools, some bubble, and some shoot up in the air. Each has a more or less regular interval at which it erupts, so as you come back the scene has changed and some that were just bubbling are then erupting.

When we drove on the road swung to the right and came around near the back of the picture. Here we saw the Black Growler and the Minute Man geysers.

We were now on our way to Madison Junction, where the road comes through from the west entrance of the park. We went through a canyon, first on one side of the river then on the other. Fine mountain scenery. The Chocolate Pots were queer. They are little hot springs and they have built up little cones; their sides are brown either from iron compounds or from algae.

Gibbon Falls is on the left near the top of the pass. The water falls about eighty feet.

At Madison Junction the Gibbon and Firehole

Rivers join the Madison which flows off to the southwest to join the Missouri. Here in this meadow the discoverers of the park sat before their campfire in 1870 and planned to make this a national park.

We took the road to the south, up the Firehole River.

There is a river that is swift and tumbles and pushes and stumbles and falls on its way down.

The road is above the river and we could look down on it for several miles.

Soon we came to the Lower or Fountain Geyser Basin; that is, it was to the left of the road we were on as we did not turn off on the road that would take us past those geysers — did not know that we should have done so until afterwards. People that look at maps and guide books so much that they see nothing else are silly, but maybe knowing enough about each road so one can make a sensible choice would be better in many cases than just guessing; so there may be a middle ground.

Next we came to the far-famed Upper Geyser Basin.

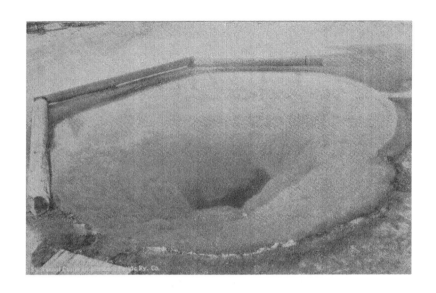

This is the first thing we saw in this region. It is called Morning Glory Pool. It is about twenty feet across, funnel-shaped, and so blue.

This basin is only about a mile long north and south and a half mile east and west but in this space are some of the finest geysers of the world.

Castle Geyser and Crested Pool

Castle Geyser in eruption.

Oblong Geyser between eruptions.

Grotto Geyser. It was erupting when we saw it. Its eruptions are from two to five hours apart. The cone is distinctive.

Giant Geyser. Height of eruption 250 feet. Erupts only once or twice a month. Seen in eruption from a distance.

The new geyser was named "The Imperial" the day we were there. The vent opened up in 1929.

We got to Old Faithful Camp about one o'clock. It was raining. We bought some food and got us a cabin. This is the largest camp in the Park. We rested a while after dinner then went down to see Old Faithful erupt.

It is not the largest geyser in the park from the point of height of eruption, length of play, or amount of water thrown out, but it is "faithful". It erupts on the average of every sixty-five minutes — never oftener than sixty or more than seventy-two minutes.

After supper we went to the bear-pits to watch the grizzlies feed. The garbage from the lodge and hotel is put on trays and the bears come there to feed. Grizzlies are much larger than black bears, their fur is silver-tipped, they are high in the shoulders. A full grown one will weigh from nine to eleven hundred pounds. They are dangerous so a ranger stands on guard with a gun while they are feeding, and people are not allowed very near there. They are nocturnal in habit so are seldom seen in the daytime.

A ranger talked about bears from horseback while they were eating. It was a good talk.

From there we went to the museum and heard a lecture about the geology of the park. The ranger had colored slides to illustrate his talk but it wasn't so good — poorly organized — maybe he couldn't help it. Then perhaps we had been talked to enough.

Then we went to see Old Faithful again. It was about ten o'clock and dark. They turned a giant spot-light upon it.

What a sight.

Then back to our cabin to bed.

FRIDAY - AUGUST 2nd

We left Old Faithful quite early in the morning. The road continues up the Firehole River for a few miles and then up Spring Creek through a canyon. The way is narrow and uphill. About eight miles from Old Faithful we crossed the Continental Divide, that is, we crossed over on to the Pacific side. Then about seven miles farther we crossed it again.

Twice we were held up by bears in narrow rocky places.

After crossing the divide the second time and going down Corkscrew Hill the road descended rapidly to Lake Junction which is a settlement on the western side of Yellowstone Lake.

Here we stopped and the girls bought some things. Lucy bought a Yellowstone pennant for the car and we pinned it across one of the windows. When we got back into the middle west people stared at us. It worried us for a while until we finally decided that they were looking at the pennant and perhaps thinking how brave or foolish it was for three unprotected females to romp off so far.

From West Thumb we were on our way out of the park. We went by way of Lewis Lake and Lewis River. Lewis and Clark came though here when they were exploring the Louisiana Purchase. We crossed the Continental Divide again over on to the Pacific side again. Once in a while we could see the Grand Tetons, hazy and blue, but getting more definite in outline.

It was over.

There are no buildings at that entrance except a small ranger station. The rangers took our little blue permit and we drove through. We stopped there and ate our lunch although there are no conveniences there.

It wasn't long before we came to Jackson Lake and the Tetons. The Tetons are out-croppings of granite.

They start in low peaks just south of the park and get higher and higher until about twenty-five miles farther south they rise abruptly over seven thousand feet from the surface of Jackson Lake. They were covered with snow and there are glaciers among their many peaks and spires. They are so imposing and so majestic that they seem more like a picture than as if one were truly seeing them.

The country east of the lake is a gently rolling plateau with park-like open places thickly grown with grass and flowers between forest patches.

We stopped at Moran where I got a patch put on the top of the car. There is a big dam here that furnishes water for irrigation west of the Tetons in Idaho. Here we paid 38 cents a gallon for gas and 40 cents for oil which was the highest yet.

For some time the country continued to alternate between high rolling plateau and mountain and open glades with forests. The flowers are beautiful, Indian paint-brushes and bluets, and many that I don't know the name of.

We crossed back soon to the Atlantic side of the Continental Divide at Togwatee Pass in a long hard climb.

About six o'clock we came to Duboise where we expected to stay all night. It was the only town we had passed all day, just a filling station here and there — and very far from here to there at that. But they were having a rodeo here and positively every place that we could stay was filled up. It gives you a queer feeling when there is no room for you anywhere and no one cares if there isn't. I enquired at the garage how far it would be before we would come to a place to stay and the garage man said eighty-seven miles. That didn't seem possible as there were names on the map nearer that that, but he pointed them out to me, one a store, one a cross-road, one a post office, one a dam, etc, and that is all a name on a map of Wyoming means. Of course, he had a right to feel peeved because I had doubted his word in the first place. But he needn't have enjoyed proving that he was right so much.

It was time to eat, but I felt so down in the depths, I couldn't. If I had to drive eighty-seven miles in the dark over those narrow twisting roads we wouldn't need a place to stay for the night as it would be morning when we got there. It would soon be dark now, we went on when I found the way out of town, all of us feeling pretty far under.

In about twelve miles we came to a ranch house in a little irrigated valley that advertised room to rent. In the mood we were in we were most afraid to try it. The lady said we could stay. We got us a little supper on her kitchen stove while she was washing her dishes.

Their names are Anderson. There are five children: John, "Sister", Kelly, Beth and baby Jane aged ten weeks. John is nearly six. Afterwards when all the children were in bed except John, we talked. She used to teach school in Wisconsin. Soon we went to bed in clean white sheets, with the sound of the water of the irrigating ditch rushing by the window.

SATURDAY - AUGUST 3rd

As it was Saturday and Mrs. Anderson had her cleaning and baking to do we decided not to bother her by getting breakfast there, but to get it at the first good place we came to.

We did not come to any good place. We stopped and cooked our breakfast at Crowheart, "population 8; altitude plenty high" is what it said on the sign situated at what I suppose is the city limits. We had to set our *stove on the ground and guard it from the depredations of Plymouth Rock hens, but it was a fine breakfast.*

We were now out into the sage-brush plains again, turning out around and twisting in be-tween hills like those in the picture, then seeing the road stretch miles ahead across an arid plain.

We saw some cattle, always Herefords, but not many. It was too dry for them to get anything to eat there and they were back up in among the hills farther, I think, because Wyoming ships lots of beef cattle east.

We were following the national highway

but it didn't mean much as there is only one sign to about every twenty-five miles, but that does not matter as there is no other road and no cross roads.

I wish somebody would take all the big advertising signs that spoil beautiful views along main traveled highways and move them along this road; it would help to keep it from seeming so lonely. I actually would have been glad to have seen one.

Even this much water rested the eye, but it wasn't often we saw even that. We met a car in the only mud-puddle in the whole road. I didn't see it at the time and I never have understood how it got there; but we got the worst of the encounter, and the Star will bear the marks of where the thick gooh came in the window and splashed upon the top to its dying day.

We ate our lunch in Lander at the pavilion in the city park. It was the only town we went through in all forenoon. We bought a lemon pie (very unusual in our diet) from the lady that took care of the building, but it was almost too hot to eat anything.

After lunch more sage brush, more foothills with twisty turns coming down them, (up them too, for that matter) more vast level places with far distant horizons, more Wyoming.

If ever I read again that this is a state covering an immense area with a very sparse population, it will certainly mean something besides words to me.

Along in the afternoon I commenced to pass and be passed by an Essex coach with a New York license plate. We had seen the people several times before. They had been just across the street from us at Canyon and had given me a piece of ice in the morning. There was a man, big, but pudgy, who wore his lodge emblem (moose or elk tooth) across his front; his wife, a thin little old lady who ought never to have worn knickers, she just didn't belong in them; and a daughter. The daughter drove. She drove fast over the grades and then stopped and cooled her engine; I drove steadily but did not need to stop; that is why we passed several times.

I hit a sharp stone in the road. Who-o-oo-sh, wobble, thump, thump, another flat. We had had one in the morning which had been fixed at Lander. The folks in the Essex stopped and the man changed the tire for us. They had a son near Casper who owns nearly two thousand acres of land, but his father wouldn't trade him his five acres in Santa Barbara N. Y. for all of it. I knew he wouldn't just from looking at him. They were nice people.

From then on I did not dare draw a deep breath or even lean back in my seat for fear that another tire would go flat. We had to go so far to find a place to get that one fixed and it was so hot.

Finally we came to a gas pump and a little lunch stand. We asked the man if he would fix the tire and he said he would try to although he did not have many tools.

A charming lady with beautiful white hair came out and invited us in out of the heat. She was born and lived as a girl and young woman in Boston. (They had just got their mail and the current number of the Atlantic Monthly lay on the table). She was lovely, but could not see why the people back in the east should have such queer ideas about Wyoming. She said, "They even asked me how we got any music out here. How ridiculous their notions are of this country." I wonder how she did get her music. I think she must have heard operas when she was young. But I didn't ask. She regretted the passing of the time when it was safe to leave the ranch house open when you went away so that it would be a place of refuge for people in need of shelter; they still leave theirs open back in the hills, but things had been stolen from it lately.

Harold was having a hard time with the tire as he had no pump and neither had I. Harold was her son's name. He looked some like a Harold in spite of his cowboy clothes; but he also looked as if other cowboys might perhaps call him Buck or something similar and that he would see to it that no one laughed at the name of Harold. He finally wangled a pump from some men who were passing. We bought a lunch there and decided to drive the ninety miles to Rawlins without stopping to eat again. It was nearly five when we left.

About twenty miles from Rawlins we came out on to a

regular eastern road, wide, rounded curves, if any, and nice little white fences where ever there was a two foot drop from the roadbed to the ditch.

Yet several cars had ruined themselves by knocking over the little fence and falling into the ditch. Why so few accidents on dangerous roads and so many where the surveyor and engineers make them as safe as they yet know how? I wonder. It was dark when we got to Rawlins, between nine and ten. It was hard to find our way into the town at night. The big camps were filled up; but we found this converted chicken coop beside a store and it was a place to stay and not too bad a one at that.

S U N D A Y - A U G U S T 4th

The girls got up and went to church at eight o'clock. I got up later and went and got the car greased. It took quite a while as it was dry. So it was nearly ten when I got back to our "cabin". They served me a good hot breakfast before we left.

We were now on the Lincoln Highway, and there was plenty of traffic going both ways. The road would be good for a ways and then there would be a great hole all across that would be impossible to miss. These alternated, but with no regularity, so it was bumpy riding.

Near Rawlins is Parco, where there is a large refining plant. It looks like a town built around a single *industry, houses alike — and stores, theater, and every-thing, on the same architectural plan and so plainly of the same date. There is a lot of oil in Wyoming.*

We went though Fort Steele. I don't believe soldiers are quartered there now, but it looks so like the illustrations in history books in the chapter that has to do with western expansion. Also like the illustrations of stories that have pony express men, bull freighters, pioneers, and scouts for their characters.

We ate our lunch a short distance out of Rock River in a very rustic cook house at a fishing camp on the river. The old grandma that belonged there came out and talked to us. She wore a sunbonnet, had no teeth, was eighty-seven years old and still did the family washing. I wonder if she smoked a pipe. She looked like the old ladies of the Ozarks who do.

We had some pavement into Laramie — a luxury. The State University is there. We went by it.

Liberal Arts Building and Women's Hall, University of Wyoming, Laramie

We had our final mountain climbing a little beyond here when we crossed the Laramie Range. Grades are quite steep, but most of these mountains are wooded. They seem to be made up of some kind of red soil.

We came to Cheyenne about six o'clock. We saw the Capitol down to the end of a cross street.

A speeding car nearly tipped over in passing us.

We were now following the railroad again. We had not seen one for quite a while.

We got a fine cabin at a camp on the eastern side of town. It had an electric stove, cupboards, and fine beds. We had come 187 miles even though the driving day had been short.

MONDAY - AUGUST 5th

We had about forty miles of Wyoming yet to do and we crossed into Nebraska a little way past Pine Bluffs. Small towns are close together along here. When we were at Big Springs we were only about nine miles from Colorado. At Big Springs we commenced to follow the Platte River, that is, the South Fork of it. We did not see the river often ... just the bluffs over to our right and the river was beyond them.

At North Platte the two forks come together. Here covered wagons used to ford the river. They say that sometimes articles are still found, covered up by the sands along the shore, that were thrown away by people in the attempt to make their loads lighter to get across.

They were putting in a piece of pavement east of here and we had a long detour, way around and about.

All day it was very hot and after driving 290 miles we were at Gothenburg.

We inquired at two camps for a place to stay, and finally got a place at the camp on the eastern side of town. It was small and dusty with only one bed, but I put up the cot in the part where the car was supposed to be driven into.

TUESDAY - AUGUST 6th

Because the Lincoln Highway is between five and six hundred miles long through Nebraska we had a long way to go yet.

The western part of Nebraska is arid, but along the Platte there is irrigation.

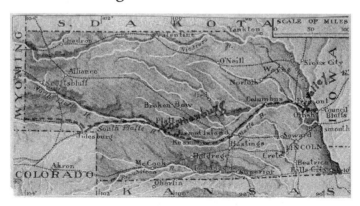

They raise grain, wheat, oats, etc, some corn; a lot of it farther east, cattle and hogs.

But in the central western part they raise alfalfa and more alfalfa, miles and miles of it.

Great stacks of hay are standing in the fields.

Machine for gathering and stacking hay is called a bull-rake.

Farther east there is the wheat belt. The road is along the Union Pacific railroad. Every little town has three or four elevators. When we were along they were trucking the threshed grain into the towns and loading it into the elevators.

Kearney, Grand Island, Columbus and Fremont are the largest towns we were through this day.

We had a late lunch as we had a hard time to find a place to eat. We had a flat tire when we stopped to eat, a piece of haywire in it. The man that ran the camp where we ate fixed it.

At night we stayed at Valley about twenty-five miles from Omaha. The camp was in charge of a man from Missouri who took considerable interest in our welfare. After supper we went up town to do some shopping and to hear the band.

WEDNESDAY - AUGUST 7th

There is a water tank on the railroad just in front of this camp and trains kept taking on water and letting off steam every little while all night. In the early morning the lady in the cabin to the right sang hymns. So we got an early start.

We had pavement to Omaha. It is a large city, but we had no trouble in getting through it.

The Lincoln Highway goes through the down town sections and the traffic was heavy.

We crossed the Missouri here and were then in Council Bluffs, Iowa.

Nebraska lay behind us.

The Lincoln Highway swings to the north here and as we had decided not to go by way of Chicago (it being our desire to visit that city when we could afford to stay at a hotel and go to some large theaters, etc.) we took but were almost immediately shunted off on to a detour and had poor roads nearly all forenoon.

Iowa is rolling prairie and we went by corn, corn, corn; three times higher than your head and stretching away as far as eye can see on both sides of the road.

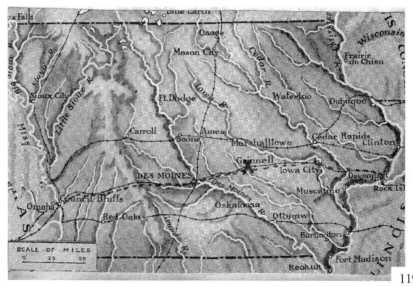

We ate our lunch in the city park at Anita. There we encountered the stout freckled young man who, with his partner, was painting Morton Salt and Coca-Cola signs all the way to the Pacific and back.

The Beautiful Capitol

We went through Des Moines in the afternoon. We went along the street that passes in front of the state capitol.

We rented a cabin at Grinnel. The starter had gone wrong. The man at the service station said it was completely done in. I was inclined to think that he was right. After the girls had the stuff unloaded I got it to start once more and took it up town. The garage man put on a new cable and some oil, charged me two dollars, and again the world was not such a bad place. I had been afraid of a big bill and it was not far to the last traveler's cheque in the "kitty".

Supper was ready when I got back and we had sweet corn, much sweet corn.

THURSDAY - AUGUST 8th

I slept on the cot as the cottage was small. I had prepared for a warm night (that is, put most of the blankets under me) but the night was cold and I had to make an adjustment during the night.

We got an early start and as we had pavement a good deal of the way now we made good time.

Physics Building, State University

At Iowa City we went by the State University. Mickey always saw all the hospitals we went by, even located the operating room if we were close enough. Lucy and I always noticed the schools; but Lucy always saw the large colleges and universities before the rest of us did.

We ate our lunch in the city park at Moscow. There were many large trees there. I had gotten into the habit of sleeping while they got the noon meal ready as we were getting anxious to get home and I was driving harder. Then, too, it makes me more sleepy to drive straight, level pavement than any other kind of road.

Iowa certainly is a wonderful farming country. I wonder if there is any more fertile region in the world. And yet I don't like it. I wonder why.

We crossed the Mississippi River at Davenport, and all of Iowa's between three and four hundred miles lay behind us.

Moline and Rock Island, Illinois are across the river.

We went through both I think, but it is hard to tell where one leaves off and the other begins.

Here we were on

but Illinois marks its state highways very well and the national highway not so well; so we followed

which is plainly marked.

Illinois is very level, and almost all of the land is

under cultivation. There are many rivers. This is a typical scene.

On the farms they raise corn and other kinds of grain and many cattle and hogs.

Besides farming regions, we passed coal mines and places where they were digging up clay to make tiles, bricks and dishes.

The only hilly places we saw were along the Illinois River. We went near Starved Rock where LaSalle build a fort. The last of the Illinois Indians perished there from starvation rather than be destroyed by the Pottawatomies.

We got into Joliet just before dark and got a place to stay.

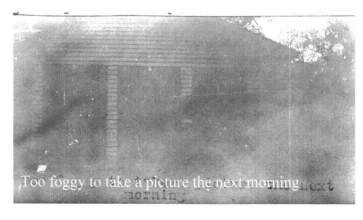

Too foggy to take a picture the next morning

We had come over three hundred miles the day before and we thought that perhaps by getting up early that we could get home by night. I thought that it would be over four hundred miles but we could try.

We took *as the road we were on went to Chicago. Small towns are close together here. Our road had been paved for many miles and we probably would have pavement until we got north of Grand Rapids. About all the roads are paved in Illinois. I don't think this black dirt makes a good road at all so that they have to be paved. We crossed many roads going to Chicago. Also many railroads.*

We crossed into Indiana while it was still quite early. Illinois lay behind us.

We saw Gary with its wide streets and its newness and its giant steel mills; and then the sand dune region and then we were through Indiana.

About forty miles was all we saw of it.

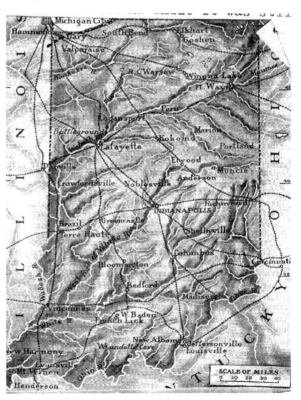

Whiteness of sand, blueness of lake, clearness of sunshine — a wilderness in the midst of civilization.

We were in MICHIGAN.

We took the road *from Chicago to Detroit. In the places where it was newly paved it was wide and fine, but in places it was narrow and lumpy and hundreds of cars from Illinois whizzed by us.*

This is the fruit belt of Michigan and every little ways there is a wayside stand with fruit and vegetables and flowers to sell. Some of them are very attractive.

We ate our lunch at St. Joseph. The park was messy and they charged for parking, but it overlooked the lake and they couldn't spoil that.

At Watervaliet we took the left hand fork in the road U.S. 31 and continued up the shore of Lake Mich-

igan as far as Holland.

There we took Michigan 21 to Grand Rapids.

We navigated its canyon of a main street all right and took U.S. 131 north. We were treading on ground that got more and more familiar although it was then about four o'clock and we were some two hundred miles from home.

We ate our supper in a County Park near Sand Lake. Then we drove on. We knew we would not find a tourist camp, but we would find a room in a home to rent. So we would drive until bed time and get as far as we could. It was rather a pleasant feeling, knowing a little about what lay ahead.

We got as far as Reed City. We had a fine room, rugs on hardwood floors, white sheets — luxuries to us.

I haven't a picture of this place. The lady's name is Mrs. Julius Affend; her house is on the corner of U.S. 10 and U.S. 131.

SATURDAY - AUGUST 10th

In the morning a tire was flat. We put on the spare, took it to a filling station, then ate our breakfast

at a restaurant (we had about four dollars in the "kitty") while it was being fixed. Then we were on the final lap.

At Alba we filled up with gas and oil for the last time and here we saw our first sign for Gaylord. It won't be long now.

We got to Amborski's and unloaded their things.

Here we parted after being together for three weeks and sharing it all together.

Here is Main Street, looking the same, per-fectly unaware that I have been away.

Here is home outwardly the same, but the occu-pants are quite aware that I have been away. Mother and Dad are all right and they surely look good to me.

Gone three weeks and an hour and a half. Traveled 4297 miles. Ninety-two cents left to wash the travel stains from the Star.

Home and glad of it.

Editor's Additions

Irene's original notebook.

 As of this year, 2006, the notebook is seventy-seven years old and the thinner paper is somewhat brittle. The attached post cards, photos and pictures she gathered, plus the wear and tear of turning pages over the rings, have made the pages quite vulnerable.

About The Star

Irene's STAR
The Yellowstone Traveler

Star was a 1922-1928 product line of Durant Motors. Durant Motors existed from 1921-1933. The web site www. DurantCars.com has extensive information on the Star auto including photos, sales catalog brochures, specifications and as well a history of the company.

The Durant Motors Automobile Club maintains a web site with other information. At their site, http://clubs.hemmings. com/frameset.cfm?club=durant , there is a nice 1926 Dealer's Brochure. From the home page select "Photographs" > "Star" . Look for the brochure in the first 1926 column.

Views
of
Irene's Star

Other early trips across the U.S.

- Cross-Canada Trip in 1923 Canadian made Star
  Automobile   http://www.geocities.com/lostnprofound/starcar.htm
- Ken Burns *Horatio's Drive*. First car trip across the U.S. (1903).
- *Lincoln Highway.* A History of the highway.
  http://www.ugcs.caltech.edu/~jlin/lincoln/history/part1.html
- *American Road* **by Pete Davies.**
  Transcontinental Motor Convey (1918)
  http://www.amazon.com/gp/product/080506883X/002-3429832-7609610?v=glance&n=283155

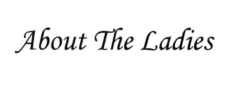

About The Ladies

Irene Angus
1900 –1974

From Miss Angus' own "no-nonsense" biography ...

❧

"Born September 27, 1900 at Paw Paw, Michigan to George and
Ramie Angus. Named Emily Irene but always called Irene.
Family moved to Otsego County in 1904.

Went to various rural and village schools, graduating from Gay-
lord High School in 1918. Taught for the next seven years
in rural schools of the county.

Did college work on Saturdays, summers, and by correspon-
dence, getting A.B. degree and Life Certificate from Central
State Teachers College (its name then) August 1926.

Taught Science in Gaylord High School for twenty years.
Taught Conservation, Chemistry and Physics in Warren
Consolidated High School, until retiring June, 1962 and
returning to Gaylord to live."

⚬⚬⚬

In 1969, a new elementary school in Warren, Michigan was named the Irene Angus Elementary School, in her honor. Quoting from the dedication program of the new school, Miss Angus *"... taught physics and chemistry and fell heir to two conservation classes which were given to her because she was from "up north" ... a term Miss Angus claims meant anywhere from Bay City to the shore of Lake Superior."*

"I have always liked the out-of-doors," said Miss Angus, "so I enjoy my conservation teaching tremendously."

"Her physics classes experimented with television in its early day of development and even then appreciated its value as a teaching device. Chemistry, however, always remained her favorite subject."

Her years of retirement were spent in poor health but her home was filled with books on a wide variety of subjects including chemistry, science, nature, poetry, etc. She enjoyed visiting with past students and friends and was always willing to tutor a child who was struggling with a subject.

Helen Murdick interviewed previous students and friends for an article in Miss Angus' home town newspaper. She said *"We came away with the feeling that Irene Angus will never want to stop learning, and being interested in all that goes on in the world. And her sense of humor is still intact, too! "*

The Amborski Sisters

Their father, Martin Ambroski, was born about 1878 in Poland. He came to the US and became a citizen as a young man. He married their mother, Mary, who was born in Trenton, Michigan. Together they raised five daughters and two sons. The children attended St. Mary's Elementary and Gaylord High School in Gaylord, Michigan.

❧

Lucy Amborski
1899—1991

While a senior Lucy took the state examination and received her certificate to teach. She attended summer school at Central State college, Mt. Pleasant, Michigan. From an Ohio newspaper article ..."*A one-room country school house was the scene of her first experience in teaching. There she taught for three years, serving as teacher, janitress, and general handy man. Every Friday she walked six miles to her home in town.*" ... "*Cooking and walking are her hobbies.*" She later graduated from Ohio State University.

According to her niece Cece Callaghan *"Aunt Lucy was teaching in the one room schoolhouse, at Big Lake near Gaylord, after having attended Normal School in Mt. Pleasant, Michigan. She taught at the Big Lake School for three years. By my calculations, in 1920 she took a summer job working as a companion/baby sitter for the McCamel family of Columbus, Ohio. They were spending the summer at a cottage on Otsego lake. Aunt Lucy was hired to care for their daughter, Bobby."*

"Dr. McCamel, head of the medical department at Ohio State University, suggested that Aunt Lucy return with them in the fall to attend the University. She took them up on the offer, living with the family during her school years there and caring for Bobby during that time. Aunt Lucy taught public school for 37 years in Columbus from 1926 to 1963. She taught history and French. After 'retiring' to Gaylord to care for our grandmother (her mother) she worked for an additional five years at St. Mary's High School. From 1967 to 1968, she also taught at the Alpine Center for handicap in Gaylord. Aunt Lucy was a remarkable woman by the standards of any day and time. It appears Irene and she were 'cut from the same cloth' and I wish I would have known Irene too."

Michaelyn "Mickey" Amborski
McKillop
1904-1989

≪✧≫

In a letter from her son G. Michael McKillop, we learn that Mickey attended Mercy Hospital Training School for Nursing in Grayling, Michigan and St. Mary's

Hospital in Grand Rapids, Michigan. She received her Michigan Registered Nurse license on January 3, 1927.

Dr. G.L. McKillop had purchased a 15-plus room mansion on Oak and Main Street and opened it as the Gaylord Hospital in 1927. Mickey worked in the hospital and she and the doctor were married in October 1929. The hospital was in operation until 1936 and remained their home until 1959. She continued to work with Dr. McKillop while they were raising their four sons: John, Robert, James (also a medical doctor), and Gordon Michael. Their home was a favorite summer vacation "adventure" according to the nieces and nephews. During those early years, her Polish heritage and ability to speak the language benefited the fairly large Polish community in Gaylord.

Mickey was a lifelong resident of Gaylord, Michigan and was active and supportive of her church, Gaylord St. Mary's and had a great interest in high school sports. She was also a Charter Member of the Gaylord Country Club.